Atlas Hour

Also by Carol Ann Davis:

Psalm

Atlas Hour

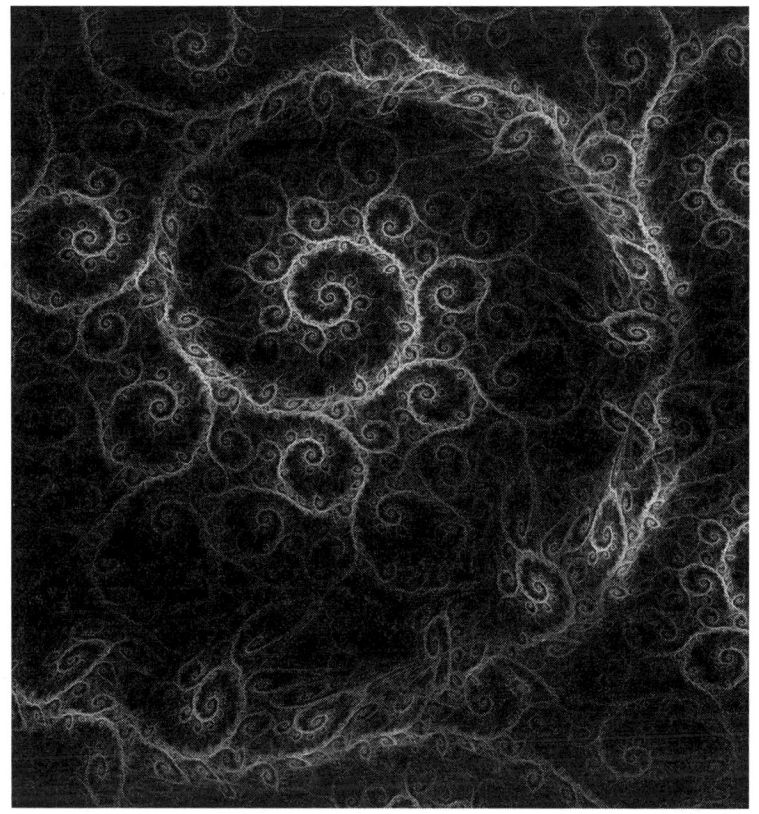

Carol Ann Davis

Poems

Tupelo Press
North Adams, Massachusetts

Library of Congress Cataloging-in-Publication Data
Davis, Carol Ann, 1970-
Atlas Hour : poems / Carol Ann Davis. – 1st pbk. ed.
    p. cm.
 ISBN 978-1-936797-00-4 (pbk. : alk. paper)
 I. Title.
 PS3604.A95578A85 2011
 811'.6--dc22

                        2011021263

Cover and text designed by Bill Kuch, WK Graphic Design.
Cover art: "I sleep only to dream of you," by Chris Trlica. Used with permission of the artist.

First paperback edition: August 2011.

Tupelo Press
P.O. Box 1767
243 Union Street, Eclipse Mill, Loft 305
North Adams, Massachusetts 01247
Telephone: (413) 664–9611 / Fax: (413) 664–9711
editor@tupelopress.org / www.tupelopress.org

Tupelo Press is an award-winning independent literary press that publishes fine fiction, nonfiction, and poetry in books that are a joy to hold as well as read. Tupelo Press is a registered 501(c)3 non-profit organization, and we rely on public support to carry out our mission of publishing extraordinary work that maybe outside the realm of large commercial publishers. Financial donations are welcome and are tax deductible.

NATIONAL ENDOWMENT FOR THE ARTS

Supported in part by an award from the National Endowment for the Arts

—for Garrett

CONTENTS

An arch, an aperture, the heavens over the arch,
what more can you want?

—*Max Weber*

 ONE

Woman Clothed in the Sun, Illuminated in the Saint-Sever Beatus

Sounds grand   but she's one of many   lost in fire   above them

spear-bearing angels   their perfect   teardrop wings

the devil below   chained at the ankle   his angels like identical twins   each

a little bored with her role   I would be too   I would not know

who to help   in the face   of so much fire   and between

the angels and the damned   a serpent's tail   out of size

joins a ring of stars   as if heaven   divided itself

from imbroglio   by star and scale   this morning   I'm wanting to tear

something out of my chest   a weight   I'm wanting

to be the woman   in the sun   no one to ask after me   no fear

of burning   but if the devil   has chosen   his few   and for no reason

or because of grace   not tied to works   I'm spared

I'm alive   outside my window   bells toll hymns   I learned

before I could read   my father's voice recalling them   from great distances

inside himself   and so the world   knits together   for a time

when the child   in the painting   asks a question   I can't read it   *puir rapt?*

when you ask for your life   do your robes burn   with the question?   here

a cool wind   a new fall   the painting   my son began

and left for me   unfinished   fireflies   the size of thumbprints and something   he once said   *flies*   *they run*   *from me*

this world blessed   with his stars and borders   inside me

this wanting   to divide   all heaven forever   from lash   and spear

Easter Unexplained

because it begins   inside affection
the afternoon's   a kept thing   the heart
blown and still   or nearly
as much of it   forgotten

as put away   so you find it
suddenly   you make a song
about *toys*   *lost by accident*
a sad list   of *plate*
and *fork*   and *knife*   and *cup*

but also   the siren that called
the firemen   to the fire   the horn
from the train   each a part
of the texture of this   each owning
its own   sure melody   inside us

at least   if to explain
that's what I'd say   I'd want something
easy to start with   the dyeing of eggs
or the girls   who hid them   well enough
to be lost   the one blue one
I hid in St. Francis' palm   how you ran up to it

bright as anything   calling it   *the live one*
and I could barely   look at you then
so sure was I   you couldn't be mine

Consolamentum (Vermeer's *Little Street*)

Its sorrows fit   on the head of a pin   *little street*   its chore-doers

visible   through open doors   back courtyards   opening

the world there   unfolds, inheres   and makes true

the sound of it   anyway   the milkmaid gone   to market   the lady

with her list of orders   bow your head   say you're sorry into it

the holy person   evaporated   into   brick on brick

the solarium   quiet   young marble-throwers   bent to tasks

like counting   like spelling   their names   or learning Latin

who's to say   where knowledge   becomes underhue   tests itself

and fades   its fine   plain-weave linen   aglow   the street

containing umber   a little chalk   and lead white   the difference

between this   and a sermon   the level   of doubt

the bent figures   their pentimento   telling us

prayer is one   of many ways   to work   and love   like regret

is azurite   part cream   part lead-tin yellow

The dream of eating

everything in the house   first the food
its boxes and cans   the refrigerator empty
save shelves and light   the books in the foyer·
to eat their spine-glue   an honored tradition actually
Russian almost   last *our toes for dessert*   so that you wake full
so that you tell the story twice   how after feasting
you were chrysalis   a cocoon finally   then an empty bag
and then for emphasis   your hands spread wide
you emerge from these sheets   *a beautiful butterfly*
this from a book   with holes in it
you've fallen asleep to   this from a want
to be hungry   or empty
maybe the way   dreams traffic   it's something else entirely
in you   a thing hard wired   and mysterious
so that when   alone with my books later
the artist   mentions heaven   I see you
flying up as you did   .   from white sheets
your room's ceiling   waterstained and bluish
an arch   *an aperture*
you would   in your hungry dream
eat first the arch   then what room
it made above you   *the heavens*
over the arch   and dreaming

teach me everything   except
the *what more*   of how to keep you here

Seeing Rothko and Thinking of Crusoe

Say it   lightly now   because you're talking   color   you're saying

don't be shy   be blue   forgive the historical   imperatives

ignore them   they are aging badly   they are lying   even to glass

nothing to be done   but fade to night   that blue-black color

so much wanted by poets   I am an *I*   then the wave

later the goat   with its throat slit   you will get there   you will want

that kind of black   the triptych in the chapel   floating   ecstatic

nowhere to sit down   to worship a little god   its eyes not yet open

story being   inadequate   an insult finally   to this black soul   which has no

shape anyway   no name   so all that is   forgiven

adumbrates   until it's   set to rest   in such a black   a tide of it

something by which   to tell time   on an island   on such and such a day

before rescue   an era slipping   under lava   *largeness*   *and exaltation*

are hollow pillars   *not to be trusted*   and wanting nothing of it   wanting to take it

all back   because you were made to be sorry   a sorry figure   and hungry   *unless they have*

at their core   *unless they*   *are filled to the point of bulging*   *with the wild*

by which you mean   this triptych   with a goat at its heart   is a god   betraying

iris   and corona   blending into   what's chemical

what you wanted   the museum   of your own   longing   your black

singing   a crude tool   with carvings on it   so much the world   taken from you

---

8

Thinking of You While Looking at a
Postcard of the Oratory in El Greco's House

If I'd come to pray, then yes,
I'd have dropped to my knees
like so many before, the girl with the eyes
deep as holes and the boy who knew. Instead
it's the velvet that makes me
start to weep, and the Christ hung ornamentally
above a toddler's wooden chair, three legs.

If I'd come to pray, perhaps you
would last longer. Or the floor slats
open to grace in the arch-shadow
a doorway makes of a room. Or as Willem says
we'd find we're all a circle—
that's how money is like the world,
coins at least. Just coins.

If praying were useful
to lift you, then consider yourself
lifted. Consider the snowmelt
and the ice, consider the bears,
nearer you than any neighbor
and sleeping soundly. Consider blessing them
as once you did me, leaning carefully
over a page. Ghost, consider it done.

In the Butterfly Room with Luke at 8 Months

I would   bless the fingers of your hand
prune stained   and prune busy
your father's sweet efforts   to feed you
when you want nothing   so much as naps
and then to wake   into the eaves of the vivarium
your brother   calling everything   *a blue morpho*
and in a way   he's right
they are dim   on one side   and brilliant
on the other   so much the rhythm
of our blue risk   and retreat
nearly native now   you look
into the owl eye   of the largest wing
as the volunteer comes   with his feather on a stick
to rouse roof sleepers   as if such a thing existing
made the world realer   or opened it   just so
earlier the dawn flight   and the cold rain
the blowout   in the coat check line
the alarm of the other patrons   at your skin's glow
rare as something kept   under glass
upstairs the magical creatures   of the sea   *from Africa*
your brother would say   all the windy way back
to the hotel room   the last leaves of fall
orange and wet   under our feet   and later
both of you having learned   of street sound   having felt the hiss
of radiator heat   on bare ankles
across town   in the warm of that room
with its vines   and pools of nectar
each in its own time   to be harvested

Glossing Luke's Watercolor

This line that knows
nothing of its origins
plays underneath them, sings out loud
blue of the divine plaything, all mist-fall
and sea green, and this is you
floating pink, *hermano*,
as your brother called you
when still you were
more thought than bone,
the open field of you
tinged yellow at one edge,
so that I think only
of lemon trees. I made a vow then
among many others
you would find cuckoos,
cloudbanks, the golden mean,
stations of the cross in stained glass
or on the cave wall, and nearby,
a water-born thing with feathers—
you the god in charge,
suddenly you the one who says
what to believe and where to go. I'll go,
I promise, even as afterthought
on the brush, your cup of water
quickly dirtying
the way sunrises must,
pigment bleeding first into circle
then crescent, you tell me,
at both ends made
to taper and disappear.

Let Me

Let me breathe this air   the neighbor girls are walking
away from the noise   of the garbage truck
the older on a razor scooter   their mother behind
each shed inside a certain   *lux*   its ancestor
in stained glass   in illumination proper

something to this moment   and to the one before
the wishing well   with the copper shavings
what Willem wished for   when no one was listening
a permanent garden   *in my room*

I want permission   to sense it   to hold my hand
over evenness   and be still
understand the dimensions   swirling here
in dust motes   of *only* and *is*

I've been thinking   leastwise of Lorca's pencil drawings
how the *naturaleza muerta*   meets its cheerful fish
to the right of center   also how much
I've loved you   as distance might   its own measure
a mystery really   chalk rubbing off

on fingers   before a message
can be read   I would like   to keep near
the soldiers   in grey and blue   set up
in your living room   the flowers I brought
to swirl in the vase   but *that's a building*
Willem says   *and that*   *a house*

Via Nomentana

(... and her body was buried close to Rome
on the Nomentan Road)

Here daylight   grows fog-blent   in the quiet ruin
of what's nearby   in the harbor   a boat called Straggler
no one hauls away   and news of boys killed
of torture   there   down the ancient road
its paving stones still roasting   in sun
they've buried her   little virgin-martyr   *St. Agnes*
outside the walls   her church grown up
where mourners   first family
then pilgrims   dug into soft rock
the book says   to be near her   on their visits
little left   to show for it
but a tile hand   reaching out of frame
lamb's wool   and a body   edged toward lilt
not so easy   to kill
it turns out   and harder   to rape
the world finds   *purity admirable*   *but difficult*
the book tells me   something easily elided
in the tone of a sermon   as if again
to lose clarity   in preservation
for her   then as now
the stigmata   of a sandal-knot
is adoration   the *circlet of gilded glass*
in the chancel   a bit like   restoration
blown dusty   and nearby it all   the blond anniversary
of my father's death   marshlands he loved
on either side   of a highway given over
to light   so like skin   on a church wall
easily   and for free   I would dig
a long time   into soft rock   to find him
belief and unbelief   changing places   to grow blind

13

So you were saying

(for George Oppen)

something about   the poem   *its object is to burst*

and easily   I follow you down   a byway   of strikeouts

and white space   so as not to lose   the lakeside fog

and the morning's expulsion   that first evening

with Mary   and later   the dream in Mexico

the rust   that starts you writing again   but here

church is out   and children play   gravel under their feet

so I almost see   a new year coming   Willem dancing

to SpongeBob   this Sunday morning   holy as ever   though I don't

darken a door   as my mother would say   recalling after many years

her father   early one Sunday   as he shined her shoes   the devotion   of it

and the ruin   *in a certain light*   *every figure in the world*   *can be considered*

a dissemblant figure   I read that somewhere   about figures in paint

but I think of you   in the end   pasting notes   on the walls

of your study   *I find I am forgetting*   *all the spoken*   *of*

about the bursting   what you gave us   staying inside

the tonal color   of an hour   and feeling

the certain texture   words gain   this humanity   so uniquely yours as if in wanting   something for everyone   you could have lost   your footing

quickly   but found   in fragments remaining   a world made

by your gaze   something holier   than poetry really

What takes my breath

is just the weight of footstep

on stair, or the moment one takes

before calling a name

as if somehow—hymnody, calumny, grace—

the world could empty

into our slightest touch,

empty itself slowly

and give over its translucence.

Something of being born in it—

or to it—so that where it is dark

we let it be dark, light, light.

Upon Seeing the Terezin Children's Drawings, Two Parts

I.

it was something   I wanted
hem of a skirt   *prehensile* and its antecedents
the story of the annunciation   told backward
and with feeling .   the wind   a little
pent up inside us   an undersea world
stitched on register paper   and drawn by a child
most of them gone now   the *house of the minute*
and a thousand sirens   calling them
toward what little protection   a devil offers
the basement   full of yard goods
the third floor   storm drain
the day on the street   we walked a little ahead
of the rain that was coming   remember
your mother   still lost somewhere
our boys barely   thought of
but safer for it   that's when I saw the detail
thought to tell you its secret   *Christ in Limbo*
a museum full of names   our own children
in an apartment   full of bees
but here   the names of the dead   so many children
their pictures   on postcards
perfect jellyfish-bunny-ears-starfish-electric-eels   it was like
listening to the music   of their childhood
or walking   out into the deepest
possible water   strange fish   if I could I would follow you
stitch your name   into history somewhere

II.

if I could   stitch your name   into history somewhere
strange fish   I would follow you   into possible water
or walk   out into the deepest
music of childhood   perfect jellyfish-bunny-ears-starfish-electric-eels
so like pictures   on postcards
but here   the names of the dead   are so many children
their dreams asleep   in an apartment   full of bees
a museum so full of names   our own children
think to tell you   *Christ in Limbo*
made safer   for seeing detail
our boys barely   thought of
your mother   still lost somewhere
in the rain that was coming   remember
the day on the street   we walked a little ahead
noticed   the third floor   storm drain
the basement   full of yard goods
saw what little protection   a devil offers
a thousand sirens   calling children
most of them gone now   the *house of the minute*
stitched on register paper   drawn by a child
and pent up inside us   an undersea world
a feeling   the wind   a little story
the annunciation   told backward
hem of a skirt   *prehensile* and its antecedents
all of it something   I wanted

Last Judgment, Illuminated in the Arroyo Beatus

To have stood   in the second level   one's neck   wrapped with rope

next to another woman   with a walking stick   and long fingers   is to

no longer want   bread   water   behind us   the future

its Siennese stars   and nearby   tomorrow's   horned wolf-devil

who doesn't eat   but points down   toward rack   wheel

or fire   we are asked   to choose   while above us

sermon-givers   and those who don't know   the underworld is   close as a sewer

below us   where the heads float   among spokes   and hub

the peacock-like   two eyes of god   festooned with shell shapes   as if   when we're gone

that's what we'll be   pigment   and figure   bird-

eye-of-the-world   the finality of all   inside us from the start   *what is man?*

a seed   these among the teachings   the direction

of last things   also how to be caught up   in clouds

rather than   your own   rich fire   not to be devil

turning the wheel   but angel   scooping   the blessed   into cloud   shape

and cloud   cover   what we need   is *a great*   *buddhafield*

to want it   is to   eat its poppies   because if   hell is a wheel

that grows an eye   heaven is this   sight-losing

 T W O

The Birth Hour

So close to dawn. So near
the snowman with the orange feet,
proximate to windstorms
and a snow's arrival.
                          So near the cornea
the sky is a shed tear. The feather
pasted into the memory book, its name
forgotten, like yours, like mine. The
hair's breath.
                          So as to be
within earshot. So as not to be heard. Put on these quiet socks,
use this, your inside voice. What did your father say?
Quiet as a church mouse. What did my mother?
Bedroom eyes.
                          Close as a series,
close as uncles, the third one, the fourth,
the one who died on the ice. Legend, as in
a key. Something about arriving first,
about rescue.
                          You will have wanted
this thing to be born, you will have counted the days
it traveled, known more
than its father knew. You will have held it
close as a second to the next thing, cell to cell,
a wall prone to rupture, its veins prone—
                                              and with all you have seen
and felt still not known.

Was what came over you

(after Emily Dickinson)

anything like this
a cold wind on the neck   an ocean of pigment

I ask because   I have no real purchase   on any of it
I'm just beginning   to find

filament-like   the shapes of things   and their masks
painful to remove   but also   undergirded with color

I remember   by virtue of falling   the green
of groundswell   as it rose under me   though remember

is a strong word for it and I'm cautioned   against such
mine happened   as I was reading

and all the dead   to say I was dead   *lie down*
to say wakeful   is a limited way   of putting it

let's say you were there   and I thought I could see you
let's say   something in you   seemed in front of me

to pale the air   it's all right   to say such things in poems
at this point   it's almost expected   to note the heaviness

of one's arms   one's head attached   as ball to string
perhaps this is near   what you meant   *for I stood up*

as long by your window   your thoughts   half space themselves
to half become   I can't imagine   but something in me

thinks *to serve*   thinks *drosophila*   *the socket behind the eye*
and is quickly blessed   not what   one means   but nearer

how one feels   supplicant's stone   in the hand
and from long kneeling   a bruise on the knee

Driving Willem to School

The room of morning, yes,
        and we are in it—steeple
next to busy road,
        cars passing us
and wires staying, or we're of it,
        almost a ladder leaning
on a wall. Almost must,
        or dreams, the sleep in your eye
the day you asked me
        what is it. Last week
so small, last week a seed
        in the palm of God.
Imagine we are smaller than
        a wristbone in spring.
Imagine the vortex
        in the river Sunday,
our passing an idea
        to and fro
for how it sounded,
        the tree long dead,
its roots like hair. All of it weathering
        the better on our watch,
the river running under. *Under,*
        you think about it now
as if for the first time,
        in the rearview half your face
periphery, half dew.

Angel of the Abyss and Locusts, Illuminated in the Silos Beatus

The one child-angel   who needs only   a spear to cast   the naked

damned   with their long fingers   into void of air   into bands of color

floats there   above locust claws   needs only a spear to start   the picture's

motion   nothing so free   as knowledge   nothing so bright

as confession   but we are done with talk   at the abyss already   and whoever stops

to blame   in Indian yellow   in green made   on a press

balances so near   a locust's tail   its tip   cuts the scalp

in such weather   who would say sorry   would admit   anything

but the fall   because surely   we are falling now   and all

we've known   up to now   of the claw   the whip   and the spear

is symbol   easily no more   than one definition   of faith

its color   so red   so orange here   you are   happy to be caught

in it   the locusts seem   at any moment   to want your taming

a saddle   a meadow   or canyon   and to know

the mountain pass   that could lead you   to plains   their Arab pattern

mathematical   something to be desired   such shapes   in wheat   in moon

so that soon you see   you are drawn   in the same hand   if not for this fall

you would be   this angel   if not for the frame   you'd escape

your eyes narrowed   like a priest's   mouth open   to teeth the point of a pencil   when the flood comes   you will want

claws and teeth   *hell*   *I will be your death*   *I will be your bite,*

hell   and if you know   it's a child talking   you also know   to kneel

The Day Blooms into Parts

(after Simone Weil)

As if in answer my hands pull at something, a voice,

and come off at the wrist. I bend forward into shade

and a single face or the breath of a dragon—I cannot tell which—

brings me near. Just like that I am overlooked by the scythe.

Like a bird that once had a use I begin to pick up grasses.

I sweep the forest floor; a part of me threaded with music

swims back used up and well spoken for. And this part with a breeze

forms into a beggar asking. I'm eaten already before my blood tells me

the germ of all crimes is within you. A part so righteous

it bends into future sun. And it's dark

as a body well-tended. A soft mud attaches to the underworld

and I am made of more than one thing,

the weed I want to take, the circle around things,

a game of clover. And the thing that eats me blooms into parts.

A Little Basket of Beautiful Apples

(for Hannah Cohoon)

They *are* beautiful this bright morning the gift of a drawing

and the stone on the table speaking to it in bird call and dog call

a bit like a sermon for doubters the basket full its asymmetry

a believing little else comes to pass but breath and appetite

faceless because *face* implies ours is a divine shape implies

what little we have is other than matter other than action or abstention

as when in the blizzard the bum from the hay bales

knocks at the door and you let him in a "winter Shaker" a faithless

needful being like us sleeping blindly in the dawn

like us nothing divine in his blood but he can work he can polish

and bend the wood the apples bloom in his iris if he stays

he will stay until snow melts and then drift off

into a damp of fields the apples glow as if goldleaf

could speak its argument of lines its stems straight

and attenuated watchful if only as aspiration

if only a bent and buried longed-for way of saying living is rot

the spirit said *they were green* *when ripe* your objects drawn

on underlid to admit disorder as if with yard goods to welcome an end of faith   in ink   on paper   to know   *I saw it*

distinctly   *it was painted*   *upon a large white sheet*   *and held*   *up over our heads*

Easter Morning with Magic Markers

This marker   in your hand   is solvent
and on special paper   · reveals   you tell me
a *butterfly's wing*   its underpinnings   colorful
though the surface   is black   *oh my colors*
you said   the moment you saw it   in the basket
the colors I wanted   that kind of gratitude   the faith of it too
the Easter bunny came   but has *no face, right?*
and how you looked   for the eggs   behind books
in your *jar of pirates*   on the sill
and finding them   was disappointed   when I told you
opening each   yields only white and yolk
and not   *another surprise*   as with the plastic ones
at school   these
the disappointments   we learn little from
the cold snaps   and waking to a cold house
so the bugs we find   are dead in the pantry
and then   when I leave you   having fled
your brother's month-old cry   I see the girls on the church lawn
covering a cross   with wildflowers
between bites   of cupcake
each stem   finding its place   in foam
I don't know   what desire   sleeps in us
to make lovely   their shivering   your natural peers
in their new dresses   your faith-loving counterparts
bells that accompany   your butterfly-wing-in-the-dark

Walking My Neighborhood and Thinking of Düsseldorf Untitled

Membranes   once surrounding   the yolk of an egg   blanch

remove the surface gloss   and put you *here*   enviro-bubble

the lost dog   with spots on his tongue   in this air   I can hear you

calling some other painter's work   *untouchable*   then adding   *mine are* here

materially   fastened   to tacks   and stretcher bars

rabbit-skin glue   plain as day   in this blue world

this black world   your drips float upward   and that's also   fact

corporeal   drip merely   remembrance of brush   your assistants

washing them   and washing   found hairs left fixed   in emulsion

the finest black   of this hour   a breeze lit   and warm

it's the frame   a fine blue   which believes in nothing   gives all

and is sorry   to admit   means and ends   the run-down

dark street   of faith   each painting   wanting something like

companionship   a lost inward space   *the push*   you said

of black on blue   surface moving   finally   *inward*   *in all directions*

a ladder   to get you here   the surface stripped   and your name attached

I'm thinking of

(after viewing the Fra Angelicoes in the Museum of San Marco, Florence)

the littler *annunciation*　　　　the one in the third cell　　　　the day we discovered that kneeling

in the door　　　the angles bloomed　　　　and doing so found　　　　the vanishing of the arcs

the way in which　　　in reverse-fandango　　　feathers on an angel's wing

like peacock eyes　　　　but not as round　　　　answered our own vanishing

answered saying yes　　　　　though on the wall　　　　　Mary's nothing

but a scared girl　　　　　　　and when I stood　　　　　　in the hallway

with you just behind　　　discovering the miracle　　　of asymptote　　　　and ray

I didn't know　　　I was pregnant　　　much less　　　understand

how it might feel　　　to live in a cell　　　the limits of a door

painted into a wall　　　　we knelt so long　　　　　we forgot

the altarpiece　　　having passed by　　　its ancient gilt　　　and gone straight up

the stairway　　　　past the big annunciation　　　with its courtyard

and blown skies　　　to the dormitories　　　and keeping our heads down　　　nothing more

than common monks　　　each of us　　forgave　　　　the other's forsaking

as an angel might　　　　the hour we spent　　　finding the oblique

and the acute　　　and the next hour　　if we didn't talk　　　in the busy square

we wondered　　　　if to receive a gift　　　　of solitude

we each　　had to be born　　in the doorway　　of a room　　wanting only paint

33

now with bells ringing   in this southern town   and you home

watching our two sons   I still feel the bruises   we found

on our knees   afterwards   and maybe   begin to know

how tiniest faith   darkens to flesh

October Parting

you're a good one for that   you said
already holding the railing   after I promised
I'd write you letters   later she'll come
after I've gone   the one   who into afternoon air
has you reading poems aloud   three times a week
who hangs the wreath   and makes you walk
the perimeter   of your house of miniatures
and thinking of her   I could say
I would have kept you   but you were a wind
not trapped not spent   waiting at the door   on a stool
appointed for that purpose   and seeing you there
how it cut deep cut new   so that
having written   *bitter sweet wreath*   I can go no further

Inside Two by Rothko

I. Untitled 1950 Blue, Red, Green

If I live here   *it's because*   *you're inside*   *and ongoing*

this thread   and frame   what can be lost   is simply everything

simply deepening a blue   unknown regret   because I was recalling

your face   or something in the decision   to die

inside it   a red   that says live   and so does the earth

shading below it   sgraffiti   scraped here   and I want

this living   to be all we talk about   though many   *any day now*

are gone   and call to us   *I shall be released*   and you're gone too

most of your life   spent leaning   against a wall   cigarette

and something on your tongue   besides what we know   this shaded green

my thought exactly   persist   or escape   almost nothing

to hold you here   nothing not   made of air   and grist   if love

is green   you became it   covered it in red   then blue

because those are   thought-layers   thoughts-to-become

the rest a drink   a remark   your aperçu   about desire   winning

laughs   but serious   and blue here   your red edge

and what it holds in   what holds it in   more than I can   listen to

or take   because   if you're blue   in front of it   it's your doing

II. Golden Yellow and Magenta (Beige, Yellow, Purple)

But no purple   here   not down   where tides hit

in orange bands   or the middle   where a purer red   exists nowhere   but

the god-heart   mind   what you had to say   about it   the *equal existence*

of the world   *engendered in the mind*   *and the world*

engendered by God   insisting on   this red finally   its halo

nearing white   something affectionate in it   joyful because

you often   went to parties   you found   on this earth   people

to love   red says so   and the yellow   I want to name it

the reality of things   *and their substance*   I want that too   all of it

nearing purple   somehow   the letter to Bernard

a list really   *4th managing*   *a fairly good time*   *6th back in N.Y. the 21st.*

Hope to find you there.   later   in print somewhere   *all things done*

with straight lines   *are not dead*   who would fight you on it   who would strike

this cloudline   invisible in its purple   so much   the point

to watch   a thing die   just to name it such   yellow that runs

and is blood   *3rd there is no rest*   *from intrigue*   *anywhere*   *on Earth*

7th bringing back some   *new stills*   in the end   what you thought

of yourself   the big mystery   you left us   *it is really a matter*   the artist

not the man   talking   *of ending this solitude*   explaining why colors

must touch   *of stretching*   *one's arms again*

Bring Me

Bring me salt. Bring me soup.   And how it felt
to ask you about the fire.   Bless the blown morsel.
The burned one.   The fly eye.   The tin bird
with the mechanism   under the wings.   Rapture
so close to the tongue,   judgment
so much a part of it.   *Bring me*
his head on a platter.   I know that feeling,
I begin inside it   a set of confessions
fit only   for a dog's ear.   Within the sound
of my voice   the apples are ripening
the pupae stirring   and all manner of life forms
we grow to keep near.   Tomatoes especially,
the Joseph's Fields   fieldhands   easily our own children
the acrobats too   in the park with their ropes
and their map of the world   its long train
so alive inside us   to admit it
is to go on wanting   this blister
of a heart.

Triptych for *October 18, 1977* by Gerhard Richter

I. Hanged (*Erhangte*)
        (*to Gudrun Ensslin*)

If in your nearest   inside
you wanted   the books on the shelf
or to speak first   and often
then this apparition   not ghostly but fuzzy
speaks nothing   but the whole   pale final

the cell with window   square in the painting
the bookcase   resembling bars
and you   shadowy figure   could someone
eavesdrop on you here?   think to abide
the trickle of water through pipes   the building's
own fitful   interior   in league somehow
with you on this   last thing to be done

hanging there   they took your picture   so it's this hour
that stays   long   that fears itself
becomes paint only inasmuch   as sympathy is paint
a boy who later said   *I have kept*
this picture   *in my pocket*
to keep my hatred   *sharp*   saw you
could see you   no other way

but what's there to see   is lyric
your crescent moon face   and clutch
of hair   legs tapering
almost to   ballerina point
arms   perfect in a kind   of proportion to will

if artful   or art-made   the cord you used
was stronger than ribbon   lasted better than
the papers you hid   just before
Ulrike quit writing   her girls

II. Dead (*Tote*)

> *What have I painted? Three times Baader shot.*
> *Three times Ensslin hanged. Three times the head*
> *of the dead Meinhof after they cut her down.*
> —Gerhard Richter

Ulrike   you went first   or were taken
and now here you are   three times called back
shadow-blurred and   shadow-owned   towel marks
on the small neck   something of   the ecstatic about you
monstrance of   boyish hair

devotional of   a bared neck
you were caught   on film-then-paint
so fundamentally   untrue
so lovely   we say   you're ours to look at
ours to know   in past and future

the puckish head of the suicide   three times bathed
in monochromes   three times
placed   and disappearing   I was thinking
Madonna   when I saw your plaintive mouth

I was wanting   something of fullness for you
a kind of documentary   evidence
you'd lived before   your life was pieta and cell
source image   and autopsy
a code with which   to argue ideology

I was placing you   back in Hamburg   with the twins
the eating   and the writing
but you lay dead   as I learned to read
then lay dead again   for Gerhard to see finally
there is nothing   but *form*   so you're form-found
and form-born   but what moves me

(permit me to say   it moves me)
is the slight angle change   in the paintings
the way the   nose is strong at first   then demur
the fact of the towel marks   what they prove
of underpaint and source   the increasing darkness
of the slab   under your bent neck

III. Funeral (*Beerdigung*)

> *Of course we have light, here.*
> *Without light we couldn't see each other.*
> *There is something lacking in me.*
> —Gerhard Richter

Blur it more   blur to nothing
the interring of the dead   no longer bleeding
on the floor of the cell   or laid out
with ligature and fundament   now winding sheet
now crosslike trees   and cello drone

three boxes   one after the other   frozen midframe
followed by   light and dark   I was going to say
followed by   mourners   what was it
the mayor of Stuttgart said   *all enmity should cease*

after death   so the solemnity   of the scene
and the sweet   articulation of sky
outline of those turned   to casket or away
their heads blurred   as if in movement

but what stays   is the one look   the private one
Gudrun gave   as she walked   out of frame
after smiling   *smiling*   at us

41

If I Am Empty

if I am empty   and this robe   a shaken relief

where will I look   for coarse love

and full body   where will I find them

wanderers in the blue   of an empty tomb

I could wait a long time   just to kiss the face

to be forgiven   of the divine   aching of everything

the forms and flame   simply held   marrow and bone

and growing inside her still   the jeweled purse

this opacity   that keeps   and makes

ingrains itself   and is forgotten

neglected   as we are   how deeply   such a thing as love

by myself or divinely   is taken out and washed

and if I have it in me   to think such thoughts   as are put there

if I incline toward that   which holds a four-headed flame

and she toward ochre and weight   readying herself to carry

if I can for a moment see   her turn her head

flame of origin   angel disguised as traveller

if I have it in me   will I   take her hand

 THREE

At This Hour

Say I am not wrong to want the two finches who ring out.

Say I've begun to lose my way—no one dies

from saying it, no one even turns in their sleep. Certainly I've fallen

into old patterns, the tile markings, the blue

of the milkmaid's apron in the painting, the boys' homework cascading

from the high table. And more—

the note saying "today I felt *moody*; I ate *very little* at lunchtime;

at nap I *slept*," that plus the hand-lettered sign

over the cafeteria freezer offering *your choice of chocolate or skim*

—it has a certain feel to it, easily it becomes *life as we know it*. Still,

there's something else. It's dawn now, the school busses flash

their warning lights. Even moments ago, I could feel it,

the sky purpling to blue, the leaves of the maple—

there's no maple but I do remember one, Japanese or red,

a companion from a dream—and there's more, just under the surface,

reticulating, pulled out to pasture, faithful in its disorder.

Or the disorder's *me*, I'm the object turning in the light,

and the two finches who know I'm alive

are turning too, very quickly—

very quickly headed they know not where.

Your Self-Portrait at Three Years Old

Here the grid gives you
a long face, pursed mouth   a lip line
that says *I know*   *I begin here*
and want to know more   and eyelashes
three to radiate above, three below—
one eye to look leastwise right
the other   straight on.
There's a smartish part to your hair,
a purple neck, and the seven blue lines   becoming
how you spell your name.
                     That day you came home
talking about   *the golden mean*
what texture meant   in terms of collage
how to outline your face
in a thick black ink. I nodded into the rearview.

Now the red cheek   blue lips
and quadrant   of forehead
equal to a math   that has us wonder
into the slim curve of a cheekbone
how first with pencil   then with paint
you took what was yours.

Adoration of the Magi

Something like   the light at this moment   how to contain   and still feel
the blue eye   of the divine   the foreign   made native
of a sudden   *the heart an egg*   that's Vallejo   the problem of negative space
not a problem really   like the year you were in Russia   or how we waited
for our son all through Italy   not knowing that's   what we were up to

we were up to the bell ringing   the swarm of flies   at the country church
the downpour   at the Etruscan Museum   and all that alabaster   in our earphones
grappa straight   to the stomach   before breakfast   then off to Venice
la chiesa   the apartment in the churchyard   and the vineyard adjacent
the dogs at night   that open window   square like a monk's cell   a pilgrim's hospice
the Florentine gypsies   who saw you were kinder   but carried no money
and the Duomo   like Django's mass for the feast   left unfinished

all those years   some sort of reason   for being   *they're all sleeping*   *so nicely*
and forever   Vallejo again   that feeling   of being haunted   and blessed
something you said   as we searched for flea markets   and news of home
then in the car once back   said again   in the free parking lot   across the river
on the steps the Japanese bride   then the African one   their pictures taken
not so long ago   really   funny to think of Willem
already with us   fighting with the waiter   over half liters

or just to think of the heart expanding   in the bathroom   at La Cigale
the empty theater I walked through   its drums quiet   as you sat translating the menu
the both of you with me   as afterwards   no doubt small   no doubt glowing

Studioese (Vermeer Suite)

I. Gold-Weigher

Your dark corner   forced just so   brown of sleep

of sleeping inside   you are not young   when you   decide certain things

and not sorry   to have been born   dark blue on wine   who ever

breathed allegory   who wanted   something so foreign

or dreamed   of the translucent   inside the white?   You did

you wept inside   a white wall   you kept   secret

your pigment dreams   how a line worked   ratio of ashfall

to clear air   color seeping   through muslin   all of it your doing

oblivion   faith   the dark   and damned

historicals   we are   after all   equal parts pliable   and certain

open only   a little while   and then   to our own

inclinations   Papist's corner   and the riddle in the church   to judge

is to weigh   one thinks so   cast about   inside one's

own walls   thinks   of edges   of pure color   woman

holding a balance   there   in the upstairs room   evidence suggests

it is not gold   she weighs   but something empty   evidence

studies a catalog   counts strokes allotted   the pearl   and the nail

as we do   she waits   for the balance   to come to rest and we wish   outside the window   as light does   what she knows

soon flies up   to greet a god   who smells only   our burnt wood

II. *Woman with a Lute*

If I say   *I want to see more*   who will hear it   who will go

to the window   diffuse with shade   who will mistake her   for

so much ashfall   a mother   her own maid   she's all of those

her fingers coil   next to string   as if to forgive   is part

and parcel   the laundry not done   the cook   in a temper

something foreign   catching her attention   in the street

she's stopped her music   so as not   to be seen   heard

or so to better learn from   the argument in the alley   the scuffle

the stolen kiss   not that looking tells   not that

hearing sees   whoever's   thrown off their robe   to cover

the lion-head finial   in front of her   whoever's   stepped out of the room

owns the map   owns the lute   because what she has   she borrows

as she is borrowed from   loan of skin   to earth   a barter

struck   with the senses   because string   and pain

are universals   and in this tuning   something of the rule

of the string   that a vibration here   finds its twin   as air moves but what you make of that   what note you stall   so as to hear

what passes   below the door   what you mistake for love

what find   your map of the world   blind to   so that in saying

there is nothing here   *there is nothing*   and if crude what is heard

cuts   or burns   its hearer in the street   our lady

is entertained   our lady finds in it   a last plucked string

III. *The Music Lesson*

Her fine shoulders   interrupt   what's written

on the virginal   but please us still   the only mirror   Vermeer painted

that caught something   it wanted to hold   and below her ear

a ringlet   made of red lake   and lead-tin

above a collar   as white as   bone char   what interests her

is a key   far to the right   a difficult passage   and the woods around it

her fingers   arch and tangled   the kind of stupor   faith allows

to surround the future   *it shines*   *and makes everything shine*

outside   a priest unlocks   the church's   large red doors

and a girl throws water   at her dogs   earlier

and far from this room   something burned itself   to become white

the *auto de fe*   on streets like these   the golden cross glowing dully   to music like this   here the white water pitcher

the table carpeted   the teacher bored   and what privacy there is

inside the sound-box   left to mimic   a dog's pleading

this diffuse   dark halo   around her body

the bevel   of an hour lost   to finger play   *companion of joy*

balm of sorrow   she interrupts it   to be   made of it

but we have no such excuse   golden neck nape   so like the instrument

it bends to   as if the sun   were made of music   as if

the little faith   she's born to   were ours   and not

as we know it to be   a thing made   rather than born

IV. *Young Woman with a Water Pitcher*

How long   you've stood   studying glass-grains   or half-hearing

nothing   one hand poised   on leaded windowframe   another

on the silver pitcher   its reflected stripe   of apopleptic blue

here the storm   spits ruminatively   the water stains a wall

and we trace it with pencil   but where you are   your collar

and headpiece   are habitlike   the walls   wear thin

on bunched cloth   jewelry box   and a fine red   where shadow hits the water is cold   the day still   and how you prepare yourself

for your charge   is a mystery   to think nothing   the 500 years

you sign on for each morning   anew   maybe it's a relief

from the alternative   the yellowish map   the threads of the rug

each a metaphysics   better left   to paper eaters

and moths   nothing to learn   nothing to make   but mix

red of shade   yellow   of blue   it's a wonder

how a hand   survives its own gesturing   survives meaning   with only

scattered flake losses   abrasion   *along edges*   *and in*

thin-glazed shadows   the void of it   cracks with you

easily   as time ends   to have   lived through

absent of story   or a reason   for being   no color

helps with that   and because you never   pour that water

Mysteries of the Deep

(for Luke at six weeks)

The morning dove's cry   doubles   on the baby monitor
and the *toxic blue-ring* swims   deeply   under the town pier
this   the show we watch   to quiet you
so you see the *mimic octopus*   with your own
fish-eye   and follow the *Humboldt*   with no one to speak to
but a rigged strobe   the diver uses   flashing a phrase
into krill   the Mexicans   what is the name
for their type of fishing boat?   a *dhow* is Chinese   and a skiff
too crisp for them   they float above   sure he is
loco   to be in water   *con el Diablo*   that once
skeletonized a cow   the announcer says   which is how we feel
most mornings   1,000 feet of water below us
and no one who speaks   your language   but you
with your grunting   and your spit up
sleeping this day only   at a 45-degree angle
as mysterious   as the *flamboyant cuttlefish*   the size of your thumb
and well lit   what you will   think of us
when you can see   and your peripheral vision
no longer   flashes to blind-slats
of morning light   I have no idea   but now   like so many
unknowns   you call to me from the deep   of the next room   and I answer

53

Hide and Seek with Fresco

He calls for his brother from the top of the meadow.

Climb the hill, he says, but there is no hill.

Once he was the child who squirmed

on his mother's lap all afternoon

in a church in Sansepolcro,

maybe two eternities' worth

of red robes, his mother's fingers

blunt as kitchen knives.

Now he chases a brown pigeon

who will not be moved; he tires and asks for water.

He is a heap of flesh that must be carried.

At the top of the meadow

his brother is so much blown grass, haystacks,

a distant tower. His brother opens like a mouth, disappears.

This is not the first time he has been lost. We call, too. We say

horizon. We call because we have seen

too many worn-away frescoes; we do not know which part of the egg

we ate, the color or the wall. Brother, he calls,

then his name, into wind. It would be easier to make rain,

to take the acacia petals, burned yellow as a lizard's wrist,

and turn them to salt. It would be blindness

to want such a thing. We are bells without tongues.

We are waiting in the meadow, we call.

Willem and Rothko (Saturday Farmer's Market)

If inside the jump castle   one's shoes were off   one saw   the city
through a fine mesh   one saw   its steeples bounce   as one listened
to the choir   and thought   of yellows one knew   in close heat

one thought   of the sky   needlelike pierced   one did
of a moment   in a vague   but intentional way   know something
and fail to share it   the other bouncers   of suchwise a nature

the dolphins   surely not   listening for the high whine   of jump-castle thought
and the waves   surely calibrated   with the storm   to alight on
your slice of beach just so   just in time   for the race to the car
over red-ant sand   over the flower life cycle   just then so much   to take in

the chapel   and the book about it   the black-figure triptych   *memory*
an obstacle to clarity   one runs   from one's beginnings   whether messy   or neat
the yellow swath   of being cared for   loved   wiped with wet-naps
one forgets   until one hears   those same hymns   in cathedral bells   one sleeps finally

having hit one's head   bouncing like a monkey   having lost   one's footing
in a wave   and felt the brush   of seaweed   not knowing   its feel
its colors so fine   and other *forms*   *which are ghosts*   which find us wanting
which hum along   to the geometry of it   another obstacle   to getting blue right

this blue of sleep   of the figure   pure idea just now   above our heads
the rainbow's sphere   passing through us   its indigo ringed   with yellow
the ghost of a yellow   that loves us   and remains   by the roadside

Because today you ask

where were you   *that night*   a year ago
when you dreamed   the one nightmare
all those nights running   your father
and you   in the wave
the beach disappearing   and asking
I think you mean   *what was your dream*
I'm blank   as a fairy ring
and turn to maps   the way in which
we would name   the universe
except it's   infinite and hungry   but mostly
I want to tell you   *I was there*
at the edge of the ocean   sweeping itself
into a word I read   *the truth*   *following*
the existence   *of something*

if you are somewhere   you're swimming
and I'm here   in the same dream
thinking   if I never come back
I will be like   water
I'll still be   the water you told me of
that held you   and your father
as the shore disappeared   though who's the shore
and where it was going   I can't say now
the morning newly cold   with no nightmares to report
but the one   that left you then
and the deep   water of why   it's back now

Rothko's No. 1 (1949)

remember that   it's not   that we grow close   not that we mean

to love one another   but just   that what is bright   is common

tension   *equals*   *curbed desire*   the rooftops

where I am now   glistening   into want   or apology

the wall overhearing   a page turn   secret steeple

Good Humor man   it's easy to   admit the overblown   to want back

the now-lost   *Annunciation*   its gessoed   hands

its mosaic-laden   question of faith   the lambent   grown historical

the newborn   bright as day   a blue-yellow   so and so   inside us

it doesn't matter   what gets lost   and what hides   anymore

Portrait

It's ours   a kind of sleep   of clear attention   whether it goes well or badly

and we could be shining here   in the musty room

talk of the *guys in Southie*   with their hatch back   delivering beer & Pall Malls

made to float the way the brain   floats in water   while we

and now my face   is covered over   by the muscles of your hand

paint pools   *but individual values stay*   if you let them

the tenderness of that   and the work

the night you painted the portrait   of your friend asleep at the table

still it was all I needed   and I can see you there

before dawn   *it was a studio with a bed*

covering something over   as a child in a sheet   is covered

your brush on paper   a sound I've not heard   except in voice

then something else   *I didn't know what to do with it*   one sound made

to face another   the way color might

as you talk about the journal   *somebody gave me this beautiful book*

language for instance   or how a body turns

in the studio   each medium made up   most part

by resistance   the birdlike bodies   of the empty easels

to see them   likewise rooftops   out windows

likewise a thing   that must be waited on

the browns and blues   the way water pools

as you talk about Abel   then other things

a face   this time mine   coming and going   on the expensive paper

in the end   so much that's porous   a sieve

Atlas Hour

the flood that passed   and the wishing after it
the white dove   pecking through slate
and the window's vantage   now that the rooms are empty
now that green is everything   is all   leaves us thinking *submit*

the zero hour   is upon us   and how
almost by chance   we noticed this or that
before it was gone forever   we're never sure
what's biting the children   but the welts are there

as they sleep   *finally*   curled around bedclothes
under watercolors   they won't recall making   and stencils
I was not   *a little scared*   *when I couldn't find you*
what we've lost   what we haven't given
somehow built into   accommodated   by day itself

in this light   I'm left to hoping
you find by touch   the waxy leaves
of the magnolia   the godless oil   inside palm seeds
the *wip wip wip*   of the bird just now
donating   to its nest   our hair

So that

this late Saturday afternoon

after useless hours   we find the kite

is 2.99 at Walgreens   and the wind is right

the baby sleeping   so you choose your first one

Superman and his friends   your father recalling   the wind on the Cape

the treachery   of making one himself   out of newsprint

to work   as this one will

the cashier saying   *a good night for it*   as we leave the drugstore

you calling it   *something-greens*   and not asking for candy this once

though the sign says   *the Easter M&Ms are here*

and when we get there   the last of the beachgoers   still in their bikinis

huddle against dogwalkers   twice their age

it'd been hot earlier   we'd let that depress us   gotten dusty

in the apartment   but now you forget about wind

forget your father   and the kite

because you've found a way   to make

a path of rocks   from bits of tar   like you

spit out of the sea   etchings   still on them

shells   you've learned to name   in school

but what I like   is the gentle curve   your path makes

on the moon-pocked beach   its mimicking

a line of cheap string   that doesn't break

as it heads skyward   how just as your father does   you lose an hour.

to the task   the time it takes him

to unwind and wind   string

Daniel in the Lion's Den, Bible of 960, San Isidoro

First a glance begins   and then sweeps itself   into berry dust   does not

incline toward the winged angel   a yard bird

knows nothing of   the lions   licking at its feet   bare here

though elsewhere   he is robed   red lines

we think only flames   because we have confused   his story

with *the Hebrews*   *in the furnace*   with   *woman clothed*

in the sun   though he is stiller than she   though he stays there   in air

even as air eats him   the lions   their ribs showing

wanting nothing more   than script dissolved   into satyr   and their author

above them   a monk bent and young   his scriptorium   shady

and so far   from anywhere   our map of the world   registers a line

for his mountains   most of the peninsula   Arab by his time

but here   surrounded   by red canyon   and rivers   which bury

themselves   to braid the earth   the thin ochre   of a lion's mane   catches what

it will keep   unspools   this quiet story

along a side margin   and the frame   could be furnace   could evaporate

and burn the skin   if angels   grow beaks   and forget

every story   that swallows them   we'll know it's   because he looks

to the left   where the dove is   that he does not see   the hand that writes   *where most you abandon*   *you will stay*   if we let go

of these pages   their marrow turns   first to creature   then ash   then scent

Walking Home from the Pool

In the near dark   it takes alarm   at the smell of us

and wishing for it   creates   a sort of dusk-screen

ion-spun   and formed of nothing   it returns

as we all do   to the great ball of the sun   or it abjures

the way the moon   *is hitting the house now*   Luke says

in the manner of young children   the night grown buggy

and low but visible   his brother   runs on his own

far ahead   around the last curve before the house

how I've let him go   I'm not sure   but I squint

to find his dark matter   others too   the stories we're hearing now

of boys returned   thinner than   and afraid of their shadows

and the green hummingbird   even now making much

of my blue salvia   how big the world

and how vague   could we but touch it   well it's not worth

mentioning   this alarm sounded   at the unborn

this breath   made   it seems

entirely of catch and cover   my moon a sliver   yours a blade

and the backs of the children   as they run toward

they *do* run toward   the lit door

64

Acknowledgments

Grateful acknowledgment is made to the National Endowment for the Arts and to the College of Charleston for the awards that allowed me time to complete this book. I also thank the editors of those publications in which poems from *Atlas Hour* originally appeared or will soon appear: *AGNI Online, The American Poetry Review, Denver Quarterly, The Kenyon Review, Makeout Creek, The Southern Review, They Are Flying Planes,* and *Volt.*

I don't know how to begin thanking my husband, Garrett Doherty, for his long abidance and for the love which makes my life possible; I thank our children, Willem and Luke, for the gift of their presence and for their earliest words, which I've shamelessly borrowed throughout this book. As ever, I thank my father and mother, sister and brothers.

I thank poets Paul Allen, Elena Karina Byrne, Emily Rosko, Marjory Wentworth, and Dara Wier for their constancy and advice. I remain grateful to James Tate for his uncountable gifts over as many years. Likewise I am grateful to painter Cliffton Peacock for the studio visits that shed their light my way and into these pages. Thanks also to Gregory Kimbrell and Emilia Phillips for their eagle-eyed proofing. And to my students recent and remote—you know who you know are—who endured with grace all the weathers associated with writing this book: Thank you.

Finally, the best kind of debt, an incalculable one, is owed to the publisher of Tupelo Press, Jeffrey Levine, and his band of compatriots, Jim Schley, Rose Carlson, and Marie Gauthier, who daily perform the kinds of miracles that permit poets to spend their time writing poems knowing a press like theirs might publish them.